POSH POTATOES

COVER: *cinnamon latkes*
PREVIOUS PAGE: *Potato raisin burgers*

Posh
Potatoes

Margit Farnon-Bauer

With photographs by
Graham Goldwater

Arlington Books
King St, St James's
London

POSH POTATOES
First published 1990 by
Arlington Books (Publishers) Ltd
15–17 King Street, St James's
London SW1

© *Margit Farnon-Bauer 1990*

ISBN 0 85140 778 1

Typeset by TJB Photosetting Ltd
Grantham, Lincolnshire

Printed in Great Britain by
Martins of Berwick
Berwick upon Tweed

Bound in Great Britain by
Hunter & Foulis
Edinburgh

Contents

A Little Bit of History

Solanum Tuberosum, better known as the potato, is probably the most important plant ever to reach us from the American continent. It is believed, that the potato was first cultivated during the Aztec and Inca civilizations, around two thousand years ago.

The potato was first introduced to Europe in the mid-16th century, by explorers of that time. However it was not until the later part of the century, that its importance, not only as a food of great nutrious value, but as an easily grown vegetable, which could provide a staple diet on its own, or, as a substitute for other more expensive and less available crops, that an intensive campaign was begun, to increase its cultivation.

Today the potato is cultivated throughout the world. There is however a marked difference in its place within national or continental diets. In the U.S.A. and Great Britain, the potato is, more often than not, just thought of as a complementary food (chips etc.). But in countries such as those of central and eastern Europe, or other parts of the globe, the potato in its various forms is the mainstay of the daily diet.

Did You Know?

That Louis XVI of France, always looking for unusual jewellery, wore potato blossoms in his buttonhole.

That Frederick II (called the Great) had to post guards on his potato fields, to stop farmers removing the potatoes and throwing them onto a garbage tip.

That the Irish potato famine of 1845, caused by a parasitic fungus, led to large-scale emigration to the U.S.A., and other parts of the world.

That the potato of the 17th century, was graded a delicacy, and therefore, a prerogative of the aristocracy.

That the yearly world production is over 300 million tons, half of which comes from Europe.

That Polish vodka, almost 100% proof, is produced from potatoes.

That the Governor of Bermuda first brought the potato to North America in 1620.

Potato Varieties

(There are over 200 potato varieties grown in Great Britain)

Beginning of June – Beginning of August: Earlies

HOME GUARD:
Usually the first 'new' potato. More floury than other early varieties. Ideal for boiling and salads.

ARRAN COMET:
Grown mainly in Kent and available early in the season. A potato with a white skin and creamy flesh. Ideal for boiling and salads.

ULSTER SCEPTRE:
A good cooking potato, long oval in shape and has a white skin and flesh. Use for boiling, and salads.

MARIS BARD:
An oval-shaped potato with good cooking qualities.

PENTLAND JAVELIN:
The most widely-grown early potato. Good cooking quality.

EPICURE:
Grown in South-West Scotland, they have a distinctive flavour.

Beginning of August – Beginning of April: Second Earlies

WILJA:
Long and oval in shape with yellow flesh. Ideal for boiling.

ESTIMA:
Like Wilja, cooks extremely well.

Mid-September – End of May: Maincrop

DESIRÉE:
A red-skinned potato with yellow flesh. An excellent all-round potato, but particularly good when boiled, baked or chipped.

MARIS PIPER:
The most popular maincrop variety. Suitable for most cooking uses.

CARA:
These potatoes are large and round, ideal for baking.

PENTLAND CROWN:
A popular variety, the flesh is less floury than other maincrop varieties.

KING EDWARD:
This potato is still the most widely-known variety. The flesh is very floury, which makes it ideal for mashing, roasting, or preparing potato dough.

PENTLAND SQUIRE:
A potato with very white skin and flesh. Good cooking qualities. Ideal for baking.

ROMANO:
Like Desirée, both in appearance and cooking qualities.

To try making a salad with floury potatoes, or mashing waxy ones is asking for trouble and disappointment. So, choosing the *Right* variety is *Important!*

A Brief Checklist

FOR BOILING:	Home Guard	(June – August)
	Ulster Sceptre	(June – August)
	Pentland Javelin	(June – August)
	Maris Bard	(June – August)
	Arran Comet	(June – August)
	Estima	(August – April)
	Desirée	(September – May)
	Wilja	(August – April)
FOR SALADS:	Most Earlies	(June – August, (August – April)
FOR MASHING:	King Edward	(September – May)
	Maris Piper	(September – May)
	Desirée	(September – May)
	Romano	(September – May)
FOR BAKING:	Pentland Squire	(September – May)
	Romano	(September – May)
	Cara	(September – May)
	Pentland Crown	(September – May)
	Desirée	(September – May)
	Maris Piper	(September – May)
FOR ROASTING:	Maris Piper	(September – May
AND	King Edward	(September – May)
FOR CHIPS:	Cara	(September – May)
	Desirée	(September – May)
	Ulster Sceptre	(June – August)
	Arran Comet	(June – August)

Always take into consideration, that the flavour of a potato can vary from season to season, and from area to area, due to growing conditions.

Soups & Starters

POTATO AND PARSLEY CAKES

Ingredients

500 g (1 lb) floury potatoes
25 g (1 oz) butter
100g (4 oz) plain flour
salt

2 tbsp. fresh parsley, finely
chopped
for frying: 4 tbsp. oil

Preparation

○ Wash potatoes and cook covered in salted water for about 25–30 min., or until soft ○ Drain and allow to cool briefly ○ Peel, and, mash thoroughly ○ Add butter, salt and parsley. Mix well ○ Combine mixture with flour and form a workable dough ○ On a floured surface, roll dough out to 1 cm (approx. ½ inch) thickness, and cut into 5 cm (2 inch) squares ○ Heat oil in a frying pan, and fry cakes until crispy and golden on both sides ○ Serve hot.

Preparation time 60 minutes

Serves 4

Best eaten with grilled rashers of bacon.

OPPOSITE: *Potato and parsley cakes*

POTATO AND CHESTNUT SOUP

Ingredients

500 g (1 lb) floury
potatoes
1 onion, finely
chopped
25 g (1 oz) butter
1 l (1½ pints) vegetable
stock

250 g (10 oz) unsweetened
chestnut purée
1 small carton single cream
salt
white pepper
black pepper, freshly
ground

Preparation

○ Wash and peel potatoes and cut into cubes ○ Melt butter in a large saucepan and fry onions until translucent ○ Add potatoes, pour over stock, season with salt and pepper ○ Cover and simmer for about 25 min., or until potatoes are tender. Allow to cool ○ Purée in an electric blender, adding the chestnut purée ○ Return to saucepan and heat thoroughly. Do not boil ○ Remove from heat, stir in single cream ○ Serve hot with lots of freshly ground black pepper.

Preparation time 45 minutes

Serves 4

A delicious and creamy experience.

POTATO AND SPROUT SOUP

Ingredients

500 g (1 lb) floury potatoes
300 g (12 oz) Brussels
sprouts, cut in half
1 small onions, finely
chopped
1 l (1½ pints) vegetable
stock

1 small carton single cream
25 g (1 oz) butter
salt
black pepper, freshly
ground
4 tsp. Parmesan cheese

Preparation

○ Wash and peel potatoes and cut into wedges ○ Melt butter in a large saucepan and fry onions for a few minutes, add sprouts and continue frying for a further 3 minutes ○ Add potatoes and stock. Season to taste ○ Bring to the boil. Reduce heat. Simmer covered for about 25 min., or until potatoes are tender ○ Allow to cool and purée in an electric blender ○ Return to saucepan and heat thoroughly ○ Remove from heat, stir in single cream and adjust seasoning ○ Serve sprinkled with Parmesan cheese.

Preparation time 50 minutes

Serves 4

Serve with toasted triangles.

POTATO AND LENTIL SOUP

Ingredients

500 g (1 lb) floury
potatoes
150 g (6 oz) split red lentils
1 onion, finely chopped
2 cloves of garlic, crushed
1 l (1½ pints) vegetable
stock

25 g (1 oz) butter
4 tbsp. double cream
2 tbsp. dry sherry
salt
white pepper

Preparation

○ Wash and peel potatoes and cut into wedges ○ Melt butter in a large saucepan and fry onion and garlic for a few minutes ○ Add potatoes, lentils and stock. Season to taste ○ Bring to the boil. Reduce heat. Simmer covered for about 25 min., or until potatoes are tender ○ Allow to cool and purée in an electric blender ○ Return to saucepan and heat thoroughly. Add sherry (If you prefer substitute sherry for cider vinegar) ○ Remove from heat, stir in cream and adjust seasoning ○ Serve hot.

Preparation time 50 minutes

Serves 4

Serve with paté on toast.

POTATO AND BACON SPEARS

Ingredients

16 small new potatoes
16 rashers of smoked
streaky bacon, rindless

2 medium onions, cut into
16 wedges
for brushing: oil

Preparation

○ Wash and scrub potatoes thoroughly ○ Cook covered in salted water for about 20–25 min., or until tender ○ Drain and allow to cool ○ Wrap each potato in a rasher of bacon ○ Divide onions and potatoes between 8 wooden sticks and brush with oil ○ Grill or barbecue until crispy.

Preparation time 45 minutes

Serves 4

A lovely starter.

THICK POTATO & CAULIFLOWER SOUP

Ingredients

500 g (1 lb) floury potatoes
250 g (10 oz) cauliflower florets
2 small onions, finely chopped
1 l (1½ pints) vegetable stock
1 small carton single cream
25 g (1 oz) butter
salt
white pepper
1 tbsp. fresh parsley, finely chopped

Preparation

○ Wash and peel potatoes and cut into wedges ○ Melt butter in a large saucepan and fry onions for a few minutes ○ Add potatoes, cauliflower florets and stock. Season to taste ○ Bring to the boil. Reduce heat. Simmer covered for about 25 min., or until potatoes are tender ○ Allow to cool and purée in an electric blender ○ Return to saucepan and heat thoroughly ○ Remove from heat, stir in single cream and adjust seasoning ○ Serve hot sprinkled with parsley.

Preparation time 50 minutes

Serves 4

Lovely served with garlic bread.

THICK POTATO SKINS

Ingredients

6 large baking potatoes   for deep-frying: oil

Preparation

○ Preheat oven to 200°C/400°F/Gas Mark 6 ○ Wash and dry potatoes, and, place in oven. Bake for about 1–1½ hours, or until tender ○ Allow potatoes to cool ○ Cut each potato lengthwise into four ○ Scoop out half of the flesh. (Use excess flesh for another recipe) ○ Heat oil and fry skins until golden and crispy ○ Lift out with a slotted spoon and lay out on a kitchen towel to drain excess fat ○ Serve warm with your favourite dip.

Preparation time 2 hours

Serves 4–6

A delicious starter.

AUSTRIAN POTATO SOUP

Ingredients

750 g (1½ lb) floury
potatoes
150 g (6 oz) carrots, sliced
150 g (6 oz) leeks, sliced
75 g (3 oz) butter
2 onions, chopped
1 l (1½ pints) vegetable
stock
salt

black pepper, freshly
ground
1 tbsp. marjoram
1 tbsp. thyme
1 tbsp. caraway seeds
½ small carton single
cream
4 tbsp. croutons

Preparation

○ Wash and peel potatoes and cut into small cubes ○ Melt butter in a large saucepan and sauté onions until translucent ○ Add carrots, leeks and potatoes ○ Pour over stock, season with salt, pepper, marjoram, thyme and caraway seeds ○ Cover and simmer for about 30 min., or until vegetables are tender. Allow to cool. ○ Purée in an electric blender ○ Return to saucepan and heat thoroughly ○ Remove from heat, stir in single cream ○ Serve garnished with croutons.

Preparation time 60 minutes

Serves 4

As a winter-warmer best eaten with brown bread and butter.

BROCCOLI POTATO CREAM SOUP

Ingredients

250 g (½ lb) floury potatoes
250 g (½ lb) broccoli,
coarsely chopped
1 l (1½ pints) vegetable
stock

25 g (1 oz) butter
1 small carton single cream
salt
white pepper

Preparation

○ Wash and peel potatoes and cut into slices ○ Melt butter in a large saucepan and sauté broccoli for a few minutes ○ Add potatoes and stock. Season to taste ○ Bring to the boil. Reduce heat. Simmer covered for about 25 min., or until potatoes are tender ○ Allow to cool and purée in an electric blender ○ Return to saucepan and heat thoroughly ○ Remove from heat, stir in single cream and adjust seasoning.

Preparation time 45 minutes

Serves 4

Very tasty, serve with some French bread.

POTATO AND LEEK SOUP

Ingredients

500 g (1 lb) floury potatoes
250 g (10 oz) leeks, thinly sliced
2 onions, finely chopped
50 g (2 oz) butter
1 l (1½ pints) vegetable stock
salt

black pepper, freshly ground
1 tsp. marjoram, dried
1 tsp. thyme, dried
1 tsp. caraway seeds
1 small carton single cream
2 tbsp. Parmesan cheese

Preparation

○ Wash and peel potatoes, and cut into small cubes ○ Melt butter in a large saucepan, and sauté onions until translucent ○ Add leeks and potatoes, continue frying for a few minutes ○ Pour over stock, season with salt, pepper. Add marjoram, thyme, and caraway seeds ○ Cover and simmer for about 30 min., or until potatoes are tender. ○ Remove from heat, stir in single cream ○ Serve sprinkled with Parmesan cheese.

Preparation time 45 minutes

Serves 4

Particularly nice on a cold day.

POTATO AND GARLIC SOUP

Ingredients

750 g (1½ lb) floury potatoes
50 g (2 oz) butter
20 cloves of garlic
1 l (1½ pints) vegetable stock

½ small carton single cream
1 tsp. marjoram, dried
salt
black pepper, freshly ground

Preparation

○ Wash and peel potatoes and cut into small cubes ○ Melt butter in a large saucepan and sauté onions until translucent ○ Add potatoes and marjoram. Season with salt and pepper ○ Pour over hot stock, cover, and simmer for about 30 min., or until potatoes are tender. Allow to cool ○ Drop garlic cloves into boiling water for about 1 min. Drain, peel and chop coarsely ○ Purée soup in an electric blender, adding the garlic ○ Return soup to the saucepan and heat thoroughly ○ Remove from heat, stir in single cream ○ Serve hot.

Preparation time 45 minutes

Serves 4

Excellent with buttered toast.

POTATO BREAD

Ingredients

500 g (1 lb) floury potatoes	1 tbsp. fresh parsley, finely chopped
25 g (1 oz) butter	caraway seeds
100 g (4 oz) self-raising flour	for greasing: oil
black pepper, freshly ground	

Preparation

○ Wash potatoes and cook covered in salted water for about 25–30 min., or until soft ○ Drain and allow to cool briefly ○ Peel, and, mash thoroughly ○ Add butter, salt, pepper and parsley. Mix well ○ Combine mixture with flour and form a workable dough ○ Slightly grease a baking tray ○ Preheat oven to 220°C/425°F/Gas Mark 7 ○ On a floured surface roll dough to a circle of 16–18 cm (approx. 7 inches) in diameter ○ Place on baking tray and mark into 8 wedges. Sprinkle with caraway seeds ○ Bake for about 25–30 min., or until golden brown.

Preparation time 1 hour 15 minutes

Serves 4

Ideal with cold meat or dips.

OPPOSITE: *Potato and egg salad*

Salads

POTATO AND EGG SALAD

Ingredients

750 g (1½ lb) potatoes
175 g (7 oz) celery, sliced
2 tbsp. fresh chives, finely
chopped
3 hard-boiled eggs,
coarsely diced
125 g (5 oz) cottage cheese
120 ml (4 fl oz) mayonnaise
from a jar

4 tbsp. white wine vinegar
1 tsp. mustard powder
salt
white pepper
paprika
fresh parsley, finely
chopped

Preparation

○ Wash potatoes, peel and cut into cubes ○ Cook covered in salted water for about 8–10 min., or until just tender ○ Drain and allow to cool ○ In a large bowl combine potatoes, celery and chives ○ Whisk cottage cheese, mayonnaise, mustard powder and vinegar until blended. Season with salt and pepper ○ Pour dressing over potato mixture and toss gently ○ Chill for about 60 min. ○ Just before serving mix with diced eggs ○ Sprinkle with parsley and paprika.

Preparation time 30 minutes

Serves 4–6

Ideal for the 'hot' British Summer.

POTATO SALAD 'AUSTRIAN STYLE'

Ingredients

750 g (1½ lb) new potatoes	salt
2 onions, finely chopped	white pepper
4 tbsp. white wine vinegar	fresh parsley, finely
100 ml (4 fl oz) walnut oil	chopped

Preparation

○ Wash and scrub potatoes thoroughly ○ Cook covered in salted water for about 20–25 min., or until tender ○ Drain and immediately cut unpeeled potatoes in half and place in a large bowl ○ Pour over oil ○ Add vinegar and onions and season to taste. Toss gently ○ Serve warm sprinkled with parsley.

Preparation time 30 minutes

Serves 4–6

Especially nice with grilled meat.

POTATO AND MUSTARD SALAD

Ingredients

500 g (1 lb) potatoes	salt
1 carton soured cream	white pepper
2 tbsp. white wine vinegar	½ tsp. paprika
1 tbsp. English mustard	1 tbsp. fresh parsley, finely
1 tbsp. French mustard	chopped

Preparation

○ Wash potatoes and cook covered in salted water for about 25–30 min., or until tender ○ Drain and allow to cool ○ Peel and cut into slices, place in a bowl ○ Mix soured cream, vinegar and mustard. Season with salt and pepper ○ Pour over potatoes and toss gently ○ Allow salad to rest for about 30 min. at room temperature ○ Serve sprinkled with parsley and paprika.

Preparation time 45 minutes

Serves 4

Excellent with cold meat.

POTATO AND TUNA SALAD

Ingredients

500 g (1 lb) new potatoes
1 tin of white tuna,
drained, flaked
4 tomatoes, diced
½ cucumber, diced
1 small onion, finely
chopped

½ carton soured cream
3 tbsp. tomato ketchup
3 tbsp. olive oil
salt
black pepper, freshly
ground
1 tbsp. capers, chopped

Preparation

○ Wash and scrub potatoes thoroughly ○ Cook covered in salted water for about 20-25 min., or until tender ○ Drain and allow to cool ○ Cut potatoes into slices and place in a bowl ○ Mix soured cream, tomato ketchup and olive oil. Season with salt and pepper. Pour over potatoes ○ Add tuna, tomatoes, cucumber and onions. Toss gently ○ Allow salad to rest for about 30 min. at room temperature ○ Serve sprinkled with chopped capers.

Preparation time 35 minutes

Serves 4

You and your guests will love it!

POTATO AND BLUE CHEESE SALAD

Ingredients

500 g (1 lb) new potatoes	salt
100 g (4 oz) Blue Stilton, grated	black pepper, freshly ground
2 tbsp. white wine vinegar	1 tbsp. walnuts, chopped
3 tbsp. walnut oil	

Preparation

○ Wash and scrub potatoes thoroughly ○ Cook covered in salted water for about 20–25 min., or until tender ○ Drain and allow to cool ○ Cut potatoes into slices and place in a bowl ○ Mix vinegar, oil and cheese. Season with salt and pepper ○ Pour over potatoes and toss well ○ Allow salad to rest for about 30 min. at room temperature ○ Serve sprinkled with chopped walnuts.

Preparation time 30 minutes

Serves 4

A 'nutty' way to serve a salad.

POTATO SALAD WITH PRAWNS

Ingredients

750 g (1½ lb) new potatoes
200 g (8 oz) prawns, frozen
1 cucumber, peeled and
sliced
4 tomatoes, sliced
1 onion, finely chopped

1 tsp. English mustard
4 tbsp. white wine vinegar
4 tbsp. oil
salt
white pepper

Preparation

○ Defrost prawns ○ Wash and scrub potatoes thoroughly
○ Cook covered in salted water for about 20–25 min., or
until tender ○ Drain. (Peel if you wish) ○ In a large bowl
combine onion, vinegar, mustard, oil, salt and pepper
○ Slice potatoes, add to dressing ○ Add cucumber,
tomatoes, prawns and toss gently ○ Chill for about 60
min., adust seasoning.

Preparation time 30 minutes

Serves 4–6

Great as a starter on a bed of green salad leaves.

OPPOSITE: *Potato salad with prawns*

POTATO AND SAUSAGE SALAD

Ingredients

500 g (1 lb) new potatoes
6 pork sausages, grilled
sliced
1 red pepper, seeded,
diced
4 tbsp. natural yoghurt
4 tbsp. mayonnaise, from
a jar

1 tbsp. white wine vinegar
4 cloves of garlic, crushed
salt
black pepper, freshly
ground
1 tbsp. fresh chives, finely
chopped

Preparation

○ Wash and scrub potatoes thoroughly ○ Cook covered in salted water for about 20-25 min., or until tender ○ Drain and allow to cool ○ Cut potatoes into slices and place in a bowl ○ Mix yoghurt, mayonnaise, vinegar and garlic. Season with salt and pepper. Pour over potatoes ○ Add sausages and peppers. Toss gently ○ Allow salad to rest for about 30 min. at room temperature ○ Serve sprinkled with chives.

Preparation time 45 minutes

Serves 4

Very nice with crusty bread.

POTATO SALAD WITH HAM

Ingredients

750 g (1½ lb) potatoes
300 g (12 oz) frozen peas
300 g (12 oz) smoked ham, diced
100 g (4 oz) smoked back bacon, rindless, finely chopped
1 onion, finely chopped

100 ml (4 fl oz) vegetable stock
2 tbsp. white wine vinegar
salt
2 tbsp. oil
fresh parsley, finely chopped

Preparation the day before

○ Wash potatoes and cook covered in salted water for about 25–30 min., or until tender ○ Drain and place in a bowl or a dish overnight. Do not refrigerate.

Preparation

○ Peel potatoes and cut into slices. Place in a large bowl ○ Boil frozen peas for about 3 min. Drain and allow to cool ○ Fry bacon without oil until crispy and set aside ○ Mix vinegar, salt, hot stock, and, pour over potatoes ○ Add ham, bacon, onions, peas and oil. Toss well. ○ Allow salad to rest for about 10 min. at room temperature ○ Before serving sprinkle with parsley.

Preparation time 45 minutes

Serves 4–6

An asset for every buffet.

POTATO AND BEEF SALAD

Ingredients

750 g (1½ lb) potatoes
200 g (8 oz) cooked beef,
cut into strips
2 onions, finely chopped
6 cocktail gherkins, sliced
1 carton soured cream
3 tbsp. white wine vinegar

3 tbsp. oil
salt
black pepper, freshly
ground
fresh chives, finely
chopped

Preparation

○ Wash potatoes and cook covered in salted water for about 25–30 min., or until tender ○ Drain and allow to cool ○ Peel potatoes and cut into slices. Put into a large bowl and add beef, onions and gherkins ○ Mix oil, vinegar and soured cream. Season with salt and pepper ○ Pour over salad and stir gently ○ Allow salad to rest for about 30 min. at room temperature ○ Before serving sprinkle with chives.

Preparation time 45 minutes

Serves 4

Serve with crusty French bread.

POTATO SALAD WITH CREAM

Ingredients

1 kg (2 lb) potatoes
150 g (6 oz) cooked ham,
cut into strips
4 cocktail gherkins,
chopped
2 small onions, finely
chopped
1 egg yolk

5 tbsp. oil
4 tbsp. white wine vinegar
2 cartons soured cream
salt
white pepper
fresh parsley, finely
chopped

Preparation

○ Wash potatoes and cook covered in salted water for about 25–30 min., or until tender ○ Drain and allow to cool ○ Peel potatoes and cut into slices. Put into a large bowl and add onions, ham and gherkins ○ Mix oil, vinegar, egg yolk and cream. Season with salt and pepper. Pour over salad and toss gently ○ Allow salad to rest for about 30 min. at room temperature ○ Serve sprinkled with parsley.

Preparation time 45 minutes

Serves 4–6

Ideal for parties.

Side-Dishes

PEPPER POTATO MIX

Ingredients

750 g (1½ lb) potatoes,	3 tbsp. oil
100 g (4 oz) smoked streaky	salt
bacon, rinded, finely	white pepper
chopped	paprika
2 onions, finely chopped	fresh chives, finely
1 green pepper, seeded and	chopped
diced	
1 red pepper, seeded and	
diced	

Preparation

○ Wash potatoes and cook covered in salted water for about 25–30 min., or until tender ○ Drain and allow to cool ○ Peel potatoes and cut into slices ○ Heat oil and sauté bacon ○ Add onions and peppers, potatoes and season with salt and pepper. Continue frying until potatoes are golden brown ○ Sprinkle with chopped chives and paprika

Preparation time 50 minutes

Serves 4

Lovely with pork sausages and fried eggs.

OPPOSITE: *Pepper potato mix*

POMMES DUCHESSE

Ingredients

750 g (1½ lb) floury potatoes
3 egg yolks
60 g (2½ oz) butter
1 tsp. salt

nutmeg, pinch
white pepper
for greasing: 1 tbsp. butter
for brushing: 1 tbsp. butter

Preparation

○ Wash and peel potatoes, cook covered in salted water for about 25–30 min., or until tender ○ Drain and allow to cool briefly ○ Mash potatoes thoroughly. Add butter and egg yolks. Season with salt, pepper and nutmeg. Mix well ○ Spoon mixture into a piping bag with a starlike nozzle and form small roses 2 inches in diameter on a greased baking tray ○ Preheat oven to 200°C/400°F/Gas Mark 6 ○ Melt butter and brush the little roses carefully with it ○ Bake for about 15 min. or until golden.

Preparation time 60 minutes

Serves 4–6

Superb with game dishes or roasts.

FRIED POTATO STICKS

Ingredients

750 g (1½ lb) floury   1 tbsp. plain flour
potatoes   1 tsp. salt
50 g (2 oz) butter   nutmeg, pinch
2 egg yolks   for frying: 4 tbsp. oil

Preparation

○ Wash potatoes and cook covered in salted water for about 25–30 min., or until tender ○ Drain and allow to cool ○ Peel, and, mash thoroughly ○ Melt butter over a very low heat, stir in egg yolks, flour, salt, nutmeg and pour over mashed potatoes ○ Knead into a workable dough ○ With floured hands form a thumb thick roll and cut roll into sticks (2 inches long) ○ Heat oil in a large frying pan and fry sticks constantly turning until golden and crispy ○ Keep warm until ready to serve.

Preparation time 60 minutes

Serves 4

Excellent with game dishes.

SAUTÉ POTATOES

Ingredients

1 kg (2 lb) potatoes
60 ml (2 fl oz) oil
50 g (2 oz) butter

salt
fresh parsley, finely
chopped

Preparation

○ Wash potatoes and cook covered in salted water for about 20 min., or until almost tender ○ Drain and allow to cool ○ Peel and cut into wedges ○ Heat oil in a large frying pan. Add butter and when butter is bubbling add potatoes ○ Fry over a moderate heat, turning occasionally, until golden brown and flaky ○ Season well with salt ○ Serve sprinkled with parsley.

Preparation time 45 minutes

Serves 4–6

Traditionally served with roasts or pies.

DRY ROAST POTATOES

Ingredients

750 g (1½ lb) potatoes,   salt
medium size

Preparation

○ Wash and peel potatoes ○ Blanch them, by putting into cold water and bringing to the boil ○ Drain thoroughly, slightly pierce the surface of each potato with a fork and sprinkle with salt ○ Preheat oven to 200°C/400°F/Gas Mark 6 ○ Place potatoes on a baking tray ○ Roast for 1–1½ hours.

Preparation time 1 hour 45 minutes

Serves 4–6

A perfect substitue for sauté potatoes.

POTATOES WITH SESAME SEEDS AND PARSLEY

Ingredients

500 g (1 lb) potatoes
75 g (3 oz) butter
salt
white pepper

3 tbsp. fresh parsley, finely chopped
3 tbsp. sesame seeds, roasted

Preparation

○ Preheat oven to 150°C/300°F/Gas Mark 2 ○ Spread sesame seeds on a flat baking tray and place in oven for about 15 min., or until golden. Toss occasionally to avoid burning ○ Wash and peel potatoes, cut into small cubes ○ Cook covered in salted water for about 8–10 min., or until just tender. Drain thoroughly ○ Melt butter in a large frying pan, add potatoes and fry until golden ○ Add parsley and sesame seeds, season with salt and pepper, and, stir gently

Preparation time 45 minutes

Serves 4

Very nice with trout, or other fish dishes.

STEAM-FRIED POTATOES

Ingredients

750 g (1½ lb) new potatoes,   50 g (2 oz) butter
very small   salt

Preparation

○ Wash and scrub potatoes thoroughly ○ Melt butter in a large frying pan (with a lid) ○ Add potatoes, cover with lid and cook covered over a low heat, for about 35 min. ○ Shake pan occasionally. But do not lift lid for the first 10 min., because the steam inside helps the cooking and prevents sticking ° Test for tenderness. Cook further if necessary ○ Sprinkle with salt.

Preparation time 45 minutes

Serves 4–6

Lovely alternative to sauté potatoes.

LYONNAISE POTATOES

Ingredients

500 g (1 lb) potatoes   chopped
2 large onions, thinly sliced   salt
125–250 ml (4–8 fl oz) milk   fresh parsley, finely
3 cloves of garlic, finely   chopped

Preparation

○ Wash and scrub potatoes thoroughly. Cut into thin slices ○ Place alternate layers of potatoes and onions in an ovenproof pie dish ○ Sprinkle chopped garlic and salt between each layer ○ Pour over enough milk to reach the top layer ○ Preheat oven to 200°C/400°F/Gas Mark 6 ○ Cook covered for about 45–60 min., or until tender ○ Serve sprinkled with parsley.

Preparation time 1 hour 15 minutes

Serves 4

Delicious with fish or chicken dishes.

POTATOES IN BECHAMEL SAUCE

Ingredients

750 g (1½ lb) potatoes,   salt
50 g (2 oz) butter   white pepper
25 g (1 oz) plain flour   sugar, pinch
350 ml (13 fl oz) milk   nutmeg, pinch
1 small carton single cream   fresh parsley, finely
1 tbsp. lemon juice   chopped

Preparation

○ Wash potatoes and cook covered in salted water for about 25–30 min., or until tender ○ Drain and allow to cool ○ Peel potatoes and cut into slices ○ Heat milk ○ Melt butter in a large saucepan, sprinkle in flour, keep stirring until slightly brown. Add hot milk and continue stirring. Cook for about 10 min. Set aside, but keep warm ○ Mix sauce with single cream and lemon juice. Season with salt, pepper, nutmeg and sugar ○ Add sliced potatoes. Reheat gently, do not cook ○ Serve sprinkled with chopped parsley.

Preparation time 50 minutes

Serves 4

How about trying it with pork sausages?

POTATOES À LA DAUPHINOISE

Ingredients

500 g (1 lb) floury
potatoes
1 tsp. salt
2 tbsp. butter
nutmeg, pinch
for the dough:
250 ml (10 fl oz) water

50 g (2 oz) butter
salt, pinch
150 g (6 oz) plain flour
4 eggs
for frying: 1 l (1½ pints) oil

Preparation

○ Wash and peel potatoes, cook covered in salted water for about 25–30 min., or until very tender ○ Drain and mash thoroughly ○ Mix with salt, nutmeg and butter ○ Bring the water to the boil, season with salt and dissolve 50 g (2 oz) butter in it. Remove from heat ○ Pour flour in to the water and stir well ○ Return saucepan to the heat, and continue stirring until mixture turns into a lump ○ Remove saucepan from heat and mix dough with one egg at a time ○ Combine potato mash and dough thoroughly ○ With floured hands form very small balls ○ Heat oil and fry until golden brown.

Preparation time 60 minutes

Serves 4

Excellent with your Sunday roast.

MASHED POTATOES

Ingredients

1 kg (2 lb) floury	salt
potatoes	nutmeg
according to taste:	fresh parsley, finely
butter	chopped
milk	

Preparation

○ Wash and peel potatoes, cook covered in salted water for about 25–30 min., or until soft ○ Heat milk ○ Drain potatoes and mash, adding milk and butter ○ Season with salt and nutmeg ○ Sprinkle with parsley.

Preparation time 35 minutes

Serves 4–6

Serve with sausages or braised liver.

POTATO CROQUETTES

Ingredients

750 g (1½ lb) floury
potatoes
1 tsp. salt
3 egg yolks
3–4 tbsp. breadcrumbs,
natural
nutmeg, pinch

for coating:
2 tbsp. plain flour
3 tbsp. breadcrumbs,
natural
2 egg whites, beaten
for frying: 500 g (1 lb) suet
or 1 l (1½ pints) oil

Preparation

○ Wash and peel potatoes, cook covered in salted water for about 25–30 min., or until tender ○ Drain and allow to cool briefly, mash thoroughly ○ Mix egg yolks and breadcrumbs into potatoes to form a workable dough. Season with salt and nutmeg ○ On a floured surface form one roll 2½ inches in diameter. Cut into 1 inch pieces. With floured hands form thumb thick rolls ○ Cover rolls firstly with flour, secondly with egg whites and thirdly with breadcrumbs ○ Heat oil (or suet) in a deep frying pan, fry croquettes for about 6 min. or until golden brown ○ Lift out with a slotted spoon and lay out on a kitchen towel to drain excess fat ○ Keep warm until ready to serve

Preparation time 60 minutes

Serves 4–6

Excellent with game, or your Sunday roast.

POTATO NUT BALLS

Ingredients

750 g (1½ lb) floury
potatoes
60 g (2½ oz) butter
3 egg yolks
1 tsp. salt

2 egg whites
100 g (4 oz) mixed nuts,
finely chopped
for frying: 1 l (1½ pints) oil

Preparation

○ Wash potatoes and cook covered in salted water for about 25–30 min., or until tender ○ Drain, and, peel immediately. Mash thoroughly ○ In a bowl whip butter and mix with egg yolks ○ Add tablespoons of potatoes and continue stirring. Season with salt ○ With floured hands knead to a workable dough (Occasionally some extra flour is needed) ○ On a floured surface form a roll 2 inches in diameter ○ Cut roll into finger thick slices and form balls ○ Heat oil in a deep frying pan to 200°C/400°F. Temperature is important! ○ Dip balls in slightly beaten egg whites and roll in chopped nuts ○ Drop balls in small numbers into the very hot oil and deep fry until golden brown ○ Lift out with a slotted spoon, and, lay out on a kitchen towel to drain excess fat ○ Keep warm until ready to serve.

Preparation time 60 minutes

Serves 4–6

Very good with fish and game dishes.

PARSLEY POTATOES

Ingredients

1 kg (2 lb) potatoes
salt
4 tbsp. butter

4 tbsp. fresh parsley,
finely chopped

Preparation

○ Wash and peel potatoes. Cut into wedges and cook covered in salted water for about 25–30 min., or until tender ○ Drain thoroughly ○ Gently melt butter in a large frying pan, add parsley and stir. Remove from heat immediately ○ Add potatoes and toss gently ○ Serve hot.

Preparation time 30 minutes

Serves 4–6

Excellent with fish and chicken dishes.

POTATOES IN OLIVE OIL

Ingredients

1 kg (2 lb) new potatoes
salt

200 ml (7 fl oz) extra virgin
olive oil

Preparation

○ Wash and scrub potatoes thoroughly ○ Cook covered in salted water for about 25–30 min., or until tender ○ Drain and slice immediately ○ Pour over oil and toss gently ○ Allow potatoes to rest for about 30 min. at room temperature. Toss occasionally.

Preparation time 30 minutes

Serves 4–6

My favourite with barbecued chicken or pork.

POTATO DISCS

Ingredients

750 g (1½ lb) potatoes,
medium size
salt

caraway seeds
for greasing: oil

Preparation

○ Preheat oven to 200°C/400°F/Gas Mark 6 ○ Wash potatoes thoroughly. Cut into slices (⅕ inch) ○ Arrange potatoes on 1–2 greased baking trays (potatoes should not overlap) ○ Sprinkle generously with salt and caraway seeds ○ Bake for about 25–30 min., or until golden.

Preparation time 35 minutes

Serves 4–6

Another excellent alternative to chips.

OPPOSITE: *Potato discs*

POTATO AND ONION MASH

Ingredients

1 kg (2 lb) floury
potatoes
1 large onion, finely
chopped
1 tbsp. oil
½ tsp. sugar

according to taste
butter
milk
salt
nutmeg

Preparation

○ Wash and peel potatoes. Cook covered in salted water
for about 25–30 min., or until soft ○ Heat the oil in a frying pan and sauté onions, sprinkle with sugar (enhances
colour) and continue frying until golden brown. Set aside
○ Heat milk ○ Drain potatoes, and, mash, adding milk
and butter. Season with salt and nutmeg ○ Stir in onions
and mix well.

Preparation time 35 minutes

Serves 4–6

Very nice with black pudding, or gammon steak.

MINTY POTATOES

Ingredients

750 g (1½ lb) potatoes
salt
1 tsp. mint, dried

1 tbsp. fresh mint,
finely chopped

Preparation

○ Wash and peel potatoes. Cut into wedges, and, cook covered in salted water for about 25–30 min., or until tender ○ For the last 5 min. of the cooking time, add dried mint ○ Drain thoroughly ○ Serve sprinkled with fresh chopped mint.

Preparation time 30 minutes

Serves 4–6

Goes very well with lamb dishes.

POTATOES IN PAPRIKA

Ingredients

750 g (1½ lb) potatoes
2 onions, finely chopped
2 cloves of garlic, finely chopped
1 green pepper, seeded, finely diced

1 tbsp. butter
1 tsp. caraway seeds
2 tsp. paprika
125 ml (5 fl oz) vegetable stock
salt

Preparation

○ Wash potatoes and cook covered in salted water for about 25–30 min., or until tender ○ Drain, peel and cut into slices ○ Melt butter in a large frying pan, sauté onions and garlic until golden ○ Add green pepper, and continue frying for 5 min ○ Mix in potatoes, paprika and caraway seeds ○ Pour hot stock over mixture, season with salt, and, simmer for about 5 min. ○ Serve warm.

Preparation time 45 minutes

Serves 4

Excellent with grilled meat.

OPPOSITE: *Potato and corned beef omelette*

Main Courses

POTATO GOULASH

Ingredients

750 g (1½ lb) potatoes
200 g (8 oz) smoked
streaky bacon, rindless,
chopped
2 onions, finely chopped
1 tbsp. paprika
1 tsp. salt

¼ tsp. cayenne pepper
1 tsp. caraway seed
400 ml (¾ pint) vegetable
stock
1 carton soured cream
for frying: 1 tbsp. oil

Preparation

○ Wash and peel potatoes, cut into ½ inch cubes ○ Place oil in a large saucepan and fry bacon, add onions and continue frying until golden ○ Add potatoes, salt, paprika and cayenne pepper, fry for another 3 min. ○ Pour over hot stock, and add caraway seeds. Stir well ○ Cook covered on medium heat for about 25–30 min., or until tender ○ Just before serving stir in soured cream.

Preparation time 45 minutes

Serves 4

With a salad, a simple, but tasty meal.

OPPOSITE: *Potato goulash*

POTATO OMELETTE

Ingredients

750 g (1½ lb) potatoes
2 onions, finely chopped
2 cloves garlic, finely chopped
6 eggs
salt

white pepper
nutmeg, pinch
fresh parsley, finely chopped
for frying: 2–3 tbsp. oil

Preparation

○ Wash potatoes and cook covered in salted water for about 25–30 min., or until tender ○ Drain and allow to cool ○ Peel and cut into slices ○ Heat oil in a large frying pan, fry onions and garlic until golden ○ Add potatoes, continue frying until golden and slightly crispy ○ Combine eggs, salt, pepper, nutmeg and beat well ○ Pour over potatoes, turn heat down, and, allow eggs to settle ○ Serve sprinkled with parsley.

Preparation time 45 minutes

Serves 4

Instead of chips with cold ham.

POTATO VEAL POT

Ingredients

750 g (1½ lb) potatoes
100 g (4 oz) leeks, thinly
sliced
250 g (10 oz) veal escalope
125 ml (5 fl oz) milk
125 ml (5 fl oz) vegetable
stock

2 tbsp. butter
1 tsp. salt
white pepper, pinch
1 tsp. marjoram, dried

Preparation the day before

○ Wash potatoes and cook covered in salted water for about 25–30 min. ○ Drain and place in a bowl or a dish overnight. Do not refrigerate.

Preparation following day

○ Peel potatoes and cut into cubes ○ Heat half the butter, and fry veal escalope until slightly brown. Remove from pan, allow to cool, and, cut into cubes ○ Preheat oven to 220°C/425°F/Gas Mark 7 ○ Melt remaining butter in an ovenproof dish and sauté leeks for about 3 min ○ Stir in potatoes, veal, salt, pepper and marjoram ○ Heat milk and stock, and, pour over potato mixture ○ Cook covered for about 15 min.

Preparation time 60 minutes

Serves 4

Serve with mixed vegetables.

POTATO AND ANCHOVY PIE

Ingredients

750 g (1½ lb) potatoes
2 tins light meat tuna, flaked
2 tins anchovies fillets, finely chopped
1 onion, finely chopped
3 tbsp. butter

125 ml (5 fl oz) water
3 tbsp. plain flour
4 tbsp. double cream
100 g (4 oz) Cheddar cheese, grated
for greasing: 1 tsp. oil

Preparation

○ Wash potatoes and cook covered in salted water for about 25–30 min., or until tender ○ Drain and allow to cool ○ Peel and cut into slices ○ Melt butter and fry onion until translucent ○ Sprinkle over flour, and continue cooking until golden ○ Pour in water and cook for 5 min. Remove from heat and stir in double cream ○ Mix tuna and anchovies ○ Preheat oven to 200°C/400°F/Gas Mark 6 ○ In a greased ovenproof dish arrange alternate layers of potatoes and fish mixture. (Start and finish with a layer of potatoes) ○ Pour over sauce, top with cheese and bake for about 30 min.

Preparation time 1 hour 15 minutes

Serves 4

As a main course serve with beetroot salad.

GNOCCHI WITH OREGANO

Ingredients

500 g (1 lb) floury	salt, pinch
potatoes	white pepper
1 egg	nutmeg, pinch
100 g (4 oz) plain flour	2 tsp. oregano

Preparation

○ Wash potatoes and cook covered in salted water for about 25–30 min., or until tender ○ Drain and allow to cool briefly ○ Peel and mash thoroughly ○ Add the beaten egg, salt, pepper, oregano and nutmeg. Mix well ○ Add flour using your hands ○ Spread smooth dough on a floured surface and cut into small squares ○ Roll each square up and then flatten slightly ○ In a large pan bring salted water to the boil ○ Drop in gnocchi and cook until they float ○ Take out with a slotted spoon ○Serve with your favourite sauce.

Preparation time 60 minutes

Serves 4

Very tasty with fresh tomato and garlic sauce.

POTATO MUSHROOM PIE

Ingredients

1 kg (2 lb) floury potatoes
500 g (1 lb) button mushrooms, cut in half
75 g (3 oz) butter
2 small cartons single cream
4 egg yolks
1 small onion, chopped
salt
pepper
nutmeg
2 tbsp. Parmesan cheese

Preparation

○ Wash and peel potatoes, cut into cubes and cook covered in salted water for about 25–30 min., or until very tender ○ Drain and mash ○ Melt 1 oz of butter and sauté mushrooms and onions for about 5 min. ○ Season with salt and pepper and remove from heat ○ Stir in 2 tbsp. single cream ○ Mix potato purée with egg yolks, remaining butter and cream. Season to taste with salt and nutmeg ○ Preheat oven to 200°C/400°F/Gas Mark 6 ○ Spoon half of potato purée into an ovenproof pie dish and top with mushroom mixture, cover with remaining potato purée. Sprinkle with Parmesan cheese ○ Bake for about 20 min.

Preparation time 60 minutes

Serves 4

Try as a main course accompanied by tomato and onion salad.

PANFRIED POTATOES WITH PRAWNS

Ingredients

500 g (1 lb) potatoes	4 eggs
250 g (10 oz) prawns, frozen	1 tbsp. soya sauce
	salt
100 g (4 oz) smoked streaky bacon, rindless, chopped	black pepper, freshly ground
1 small onion, finely chopped	fresh chives, finely chopped
3 tbsp. butter	

Preparation

○ Defrost prawns ○ Wash potatoes and cook covered in salted water for about 25–30 min., or until tender ○ Drain and allow to cool ○ Peel and cut into slices ○ Rinse prawns, and pat dry with a kitchen towel ○ Fry bacon in a large frying pan until golden ○ Add butter, onions, potatoes, prawns and continue frying until golden ○ Combine eggs, salt, pepper and soya sauce and beat well ○ Pour over potatoes, turn heat down, and, allow eggs to settle ○ Serve sprinkled with chives.

Preparation time 50 minutes

Serves 4

Goes very well with bread and butter, or serve it with fresh green salad.

POTATO & CORNED BEEF OMELETTE

Ingredients

750 g (1½ lb) potatoes
1 onion, finely chopped
6 eggs
1 tin corned beef, cubed
salt

black pepper, freshly
ground
fresh chives, finely
chopped
for frying: 2–3 tbsp. oil

Preparation

○ Wash potatoes and cook covered in salted water for about 25–30 min., or until tender ○ Drain and allow to cool ○ Peel and cut into slices ○ Heat oil in a large frying pan and fry onion until golden ○ Add corned beef and potatoes, and, continue frying until slightly crispy ○ Combine eggs, salt, pepper and chives. Beat well ○ Pour over potatoes, turn heat down, and, allow eggs to settle.

Preparation time 45 minutes

Serves 4

Just serve with some peas and carrots.

POTATO PIE

Ingredients

1½ kg (2½lb) potatoes
250 g (10 oz) cooked ham, diced
1 large onion, finely chopped
500 ml (17 fl oz) soured cream
2 tbsp. breadcrumbs, natural

100 g (4 oz) Emmental cheese, grated
1 egg
50 g (2 oz) butter
salt
white pepper

Preparation the day before

○ Wash potatoes and cook covered in salted water for about 25–30 min., or until tender ○ Drain and place in a bowl or a dish overnight. Do not refrigerate.

Preparation following day

Preheat oven to 200°C/400°F/Gas Mark 6 ○ Peel potatoes and cut into slices ○ Arrange half of potatoes in a greased ovenproof dish, top with ham, onions and finish with remaining potatoes ○ Mix soured cream, egg, salt, pepper, and, pour over potatoes ○ Sprinkle with breadcrumbs and cheese. Top with knobs of butter ○ Bake for about 40 minutes.

Preparation time 1 hour 15 minutes

Serves 4–6

Serve with a salad of your choice.

GRATIN DAUPHINOISE

Ingredients

1 kg (2 lb) potatoes	cheese, grated
2 eggs	4 tbsp. butter
2 cartons single cream	salt
200 ml (8 fl oz) milk	black pepper, freshly
6 cloves of garlic, crushed	ground
200 g (8 oz) Emmental	nutmeg, pinch

Preparation

○ Wash and peel potatoes, cut into thin slices and mix in a bowl with salt, pepper and nutmeg. ○ Slightly whisk eggs, cream and milk. Season with salt ○ Mix half the butter with crushed garlic, and spread over bottom of a large baking tray ○ Preheat oven to 200°C/400°F/Gas Mark 6 ○ Arrange potatoes (like roof-tiles) into three layers ○ Sprinkle each layer with egg and cream mixture and cheese ○ End by sprinkling top layer in the same manner, and add some knobs of butter ○ Bake for about 60 min. Cover with foil after 30 min.

Preparation time 1 hour 30 minutes

Serves 4–6

A delicious dish, which was a favourite with the French aristocracy.

ZÜRCHER RÖSTI

Ingredients

750 g (1½lb) potatoes   salt
1 large onion, grated   white pepper
75 g (3 oz) butter

Preparation the day before

○ Wash potatoes and cook covered in salted water for about 25–30 min., or until tender ○ Drain and place in a bowl or a dish overnight. Do not refrigerate.

Preparation following day

Peel potatoes and grate into a bowl ○ Gently mix with grated onion, salt and pepper ○ Melt half the butter in a large frying pan, spread potatoes evenly, and ensure mixture is level ○ Fry until a golden brown crust is forming ○ Aided by a round plate (flat lid) turn the Rösti ○ Melt second half of the butter and return Rösti to frying pan, leaving crusty side on top ○ Continue frying until second side is crusty.

Preparation time 60 minutes

Serves 4

Mouth–watering with fried eggs and a salad.

ALPINE POTATO STEW

Ingredients

500 g (1 lb) potatoes
150 g (6 oz) carrots, diced
150 g (6 oz) parsnip, diced
1 tin black eyed beans, drained
1 small onion, finely chopped
200 g (8 oz) smoked streaky bacon, rindless, finely chopped

25 g (1 oz) butter
1 l (1½ pints) vegetable stock
1 carton soured cream
1 tsp. Worcestershire sauce
½ tsp. caraway seeds
salt
black pepper, freshly ground

Preparation

○ In a small frying pan sauté bacon until golden and crispy. Drain excess fat and set aside. ○ Wash and peel potatoes and cut into cubes ○ Melt butter in a large saucepan and fry onion until translucent ○ Add potatoes, carrots, parsnip, beans and stock. Season with salt, pepper, caraway seeds and Worcestershire sauce ○ Bring to the boil. Reduce heat. Simmer covered for about 20–25 min., or until potatoes are tender ○ Just before serving stir in soured cream and remove immediately from heat ○ Serve sprinkled with bacon.

Preparation time 50 minutes

Serves 4

Just right for a cold winter evening.

SHEPHERD'S PIE

Ingredients

750 g (1½lb) floury
potatoes
500 g (1 lb) minced lamb
1 small onion, finely
chopped
4 cloves of garlic, crushed
25 g (1 oz) butter
1–2 tbsp. plain flour
125 ml (5 fl oz) vegetable
stock
2 tbsp. red wine vinegar

½ tsp. rosemary, dried
½ tsp. marjoram, dried
½ tsp. thyme, dried
salt
black pepper, freshly
ground
for greasing: ½ tsp. oil
for potato mash, according
to taste: milk, butter, salt,
nutmeg

Preparation

○ Wash and peel potatoes and and cut into wedges
○ Cook covered in salted water for about 20–25 min., or
until tender ○ Melt butter in a frying pan and sauté onion
and garlic until translucent ○ Add the flour and keep stirring for approx. a minute ○ Stir in vegetable stock and
vinegar. Season with salt, pepper, rosemary, thyme and
marjoram ○ Add the minced meat and mix well. Cover
and simmer for about 10–15 min., stirring occasionally
○ Drain potatoes, and, mash thoroughly. Add butter,
milk, salt and nutmeg according to taste ○ Spoon mashed
potatoes into a piping bag with a starlike nozzle ○ Place
meat mixture in an ovenproof dish (*slightly* greased) and
pipe potatoes on top ○ Grill or bake until lightly
browned.

Preparation time 50 minutes   Serves 4

BUBBLE AND SQUEAK

Ingredients

1 kg (2 lb) potatoes
250 g (10 oz) cabbage or
Brussels sprouts, cooked,
chopped (usually leftovers)
1 medium onion, finely
chopped

salt
25 g (1 oz) butter
black pepper, freshly
ground
for dusting: plain flour
for frying: oil

Preparation

○ Wash and peel potatoes, cook covered in salted water for about 25–30 min., or until very tender ○ Drain, and, mash thoroughly. Add butter and season well ○ Mix with cabbage or Brussels sprouts and onion ○ Form little cakes and dust them with flour ○ Heat oil in a large frying pan and fry cakes until golden and crispy on both sides ○ Lift out with a slotted spoon and lay out on a kitchen towel to drain excess fat ○ Keep warm until ready to serve.

Preparation time 60 minutes

Serves 4–6

Topped with fried eggs a tasty "leftover-meal".

COTTAGE PIE

Ingredients

750 g (1½ lb) floury potatoes
500 g (1 lb) minced beef
1 small onion, finely chopped
1 clove of garlic, crushed
25 g (1 oz) butter
2 tbsp. tomato purée
1–2 tbsp. plain flour
125 ml (5 fl oz) vegetable stock
2 tbsp. dry sherry
½ tsp. marjoram, dried

½ tsp. thyme, dried
1 tsp. paprika
¼ tsp. cayenne pepper
salt
black pepper, freshly ground
4 tbsp. Cheddar cheese, grated
for greasing: ½ tsp. oil
for potato mash, according to taste: milk, butter, salt, nutmeg

Preparation

○ Wash and peel potatoes and and cut into wedges ○ Cook covered in salted water for about 20–25 min., or until tender ○ Melt butter in a frying pan and sauté onion and garlic until translucent ○ Add the flour and keep stirring for approx. a minute ○ Stir in vegetable stock, tomato purée and sherry. Season with salt, pepper, marjoram, thyme, paprika and cayenne pepper ○ Add the minced meat and mix well. Cover and simmer for about 10–15 min., stirring occasionally ○ Drain potatoes, and, mash thoroughly. Add butter, milk, salt and nutmeg according to taste ○ Spoon mashed potatoes into a piping bag with a starlike nozzle ○ Place meat mixture in an ovenproof dish (slightly greased) and pipe potatoes on top ○ Sprinkle with cheese and grill or bake until lightly browned.

Preparation time 50 minutes   Serves 4

POTATOES IN SAVOURY SAUCE

Ingredients

750 g (1½ lb) potatoes
150 g (6 oz) smoked streaky bacon, rindless, chopped
2 onions, finely chopped
200 g (8 oz) cocktail gherkins, finely chopped
1 tbsp. plain flour
400 ml (¾ pint) vegetable stock
1 tbsp. capers
1 tbsp. white wine vinegar
½ tsp. marjoram, dried
½ tsp. thyme, dried
1 tsp. salt
black pepper, freshly ground
fresh parsley, finely chopped

Preparation

○ Wash potatoes and cook covered in salted water for about 25–30 min., or until tender ○ Drain, peel, and, cut into slices ○ In a large saucepan fry bacon, add onions and continue frying until golden ○ Sprinkle with flour, add stock and heat stirring constantly ○ Add capers, herbs, salt, pepper and vinegar ○ Stir in potatoes and gherkins and heat thoroughly ○ Serve sprinkled with parsley.

Preparation time 60 minutes

Serves 4

Try this dish with a cucumber salad.

POTATO GOUDA CHEESE LAYERS

Ingredients

1 kg (2 lb) potatoes
4 large onions, finely
chopped
1 tbsp. butter
250 g (10 oz) Gouda cheese,
grated
black pepper, freshly
ground

nutmeg
thyme, dried
salt
2 tbsp. capers, chopped
1 bunch of fresh parsley,
finely chopped
for greasing: oil

Preparation

○ Wash potatoes and cook covered in salted water for about 15 min., or until just tender ○ Drain and allow to cool ○ Peel and cut into slices ○ Preheat oven to 200°C/400°F/Gas Mark 6 ○ Melt butter in a large frying pan and cook onions until golden. Set aside ○ In a greased oven-proof dish, arrange a layer of potatoes. Sprinkle with parsley, cheese, onions, capers, thyme, salt, pepper and nutmeg. Repeat process ○ Finish top layer with all ingredients mentioned, and, sprinkle with remaining cheese ○ Bake for about 30 min.

Preparation time 60 minutes

Serves 4

With a cauliflower salad a perfect main course.

POTATO TOMATO PIE

Ingredients

750 g (1½ lb) potatoes
2 onions, sliced
500 g (1 lb) tomatoes, sliced
500 g (1 lb) beef fillet, sliced
2 tbsp. oil

100 g (4 oz) Cheddar cheese, grated
1 carton soured cream
salt
black pepper, freshly ground
½ tsp. thyme

Preparation the day before

○ Wash potatoes and cook covered in salted water for about 25–30 min., or until tender ○ Drain and place in a bowl or a dish overnight. Do not refrigerate.

Preparation following day

○ Peel potatoes and cut into slices ○ Preheat oven to 200°C/400°F/Gas Mark 6 ○ In a little bit of oil fry beef slices for 2 min. on each side. Season with salt and pepper after sealing ○ Arrange a layer of potatoes in a greased ovenproof dish and top with beef, sprinkle with remaining oil ○ Top with mixed layers of tomatoes, potatoes and onion slices ○ Sprinkle top layer with salt, pepper and thyme ○ Mix cheese and soured cream and pour over pie ○ Bake uncovered for about 15 min.

Preparation time 60 minutes

Serves 4

Serve with a fresh salad.

POTATO FISH BURGERS

Ingredients

500 g (1 lb) floury
potatoes
250 g (10 oz) smoked cod
fillets, skinned and flaked
1 small onion, finely
chopped

1 tbsp. fresh parsley, finely
chopped
1 egg
5 tbsp. breadcrumbs,
natural
for frying: oil

Preparation

○ Wash and peel potatoes, cook covered in salted water for about 25–30 min., or until soft ○ Drain, and, mash thoroughly ○ Combine potatoes with flaked fish, onion and parsley. Mix well ○ Form approx. 8 fish burgers ○ Dip firstly in slightly beaten egg and secondly in bread-crumbs ○ Heat oil and fry for about 5 min. each side or until golden ○ Serve hot.

Preparation time 50 minutes

Serves 4

Serve with mixed vegetables, or salad.

POTATO FRITTERS

Ingredients

1 kg (2 lb) floury
potatoes
1 large onion, grated
2 tbsp. plain flour

2 eggs
1 tsp. salt
4 tbsp. lard

Preparation

○ Wash and peel potatoes, grate them into a bowl of cold water ○ Squeeze grated potatoes through a muslin cloth and collect water in which the potato flour will settle. (Approx. 45 min.) ○ When potato flour has settled, carefully drain off the water, leaving the flour behind, then mix the potato flour with the grated potatoes ○ Combine this mixture with plain flour, eggs, salt and onions ○ Heat lard in a frying pan. Put 2 tbsp. of potato mixture at a time into the pan. Fry quickly on both sides until golden and crispy ○ Keep warm until ready to serve.

Preparation time 30 minutes

Serves 4–6·

Eat with a salad or baked beans.

POTATO CHIPOLATAS

Ingredients

1½ kg (3 lb) floury potatoes	3 tsp. salt 1 tbsp. marjoram, dried

Preparation

○ Wash and peel all potatoes ○ Take 500 g (1 lb) and cut into quarters. Cook covered in salted water for about 20–25 min., or until tender ○ Grate remaining 1 kg (2 lb) into a bowl of cold water ○ Squeeze grated potatoes through a muslin cloth and collect water in which the potato flour will settle (Approx. 45 min.) ○ Mash cooked potatoes thoroughly ○ When potato flour has settled, carefully drain off the water, leaving the flour behind, then mix the potato flour with mash and grated potatoes. Add 1½ tsp. salt and marjoram ○ Knead to a workable dough. (Occasionally extra flour or water is needed) ○ Bring 3 l (5 pints) of water with remaining salt to the boil ○ With wet hands form chipolatas ○ Drop into boiling water and immediately reduce heat ○ Simmer for about 20 min. (without a lid) ○ Lift out with a slotted spoon. Serve hot.

Preparation time 1 hour 15 min

Serves 4–6

Best served with a fresh tomato and garlic sauce.

POTATO AND BACON DUMPLINGS

Ingredients

1½ kg (3 lb) floury
potatoes
3 tsp. salt
200 g (8 oz) smoked streaky
bacon, rindless, chopped
2 onions, finely chopped

1–2 tbsp. plain flour
1 egg
nutmeg, pinch
2 tbsp. fresh parsley,
finely chopped

Preparation

○ Wash and peel all potatoes ○ Take 500 g (1 lb) and cut into quarters. Cook covered in salted water for about 20–25 min., or until tender ○ Grate remaining 1 kg (2 lb) into a bowl of cold water ○ Squeeze grated potatoes through a muslin cloth and collect water in which the potato flour will settle. (Approx. 45 min.) ○ Mash cooked potatoes thoroughly ○ When potato flour has settled, carefully drain off the water, leaving the flour behind, then mix the potato flour with mashed and grated potatoes ○ Fry bacon until crispy, add onions and brown slightly. Set aside ○ Combine potato mixture with flour, egg, 1 tsp. salt, nutmeg, and form a workable dough. (Occasionally extra water is needed) ○ Work in parsley, bacon and onions ○ Bring 3 l (5 pints) of water with remaining salt to the boil ○ Form a 'trial-dumpling' (small), and slip it into the boiling water, turn heat down and simmer for about 25 min. If dumpling loses its shape then add 1 tbsp. of flour to the dough ○ With wet hands form (medium size) dumplings, drop them into the boiling water, bring briefly back to boil, turn heat down and simmer for about 25–30 min. without a lid.

Preparation time 1 hour 30 minutes   Serves 4–6

Fillings & Toppings

BAKED CHEDDAR POTATOES

Ingredients

4 large baking potatoes	4 tbsp. double cream
200 g (8 oz) Cheddar	caraway seeds
cheese, grated	salt
2 tbsp. oil	pepper

Preparation

○ Preheat oven to 200°C/400°F/Gas Mark 6 ○ Wash potatoes thoroughly and cut in half ○ Prick surface with a fork and sprinkle with salt, pepper and oil ○ Arrange with flat side down on a greased baking tray ○ Bake for about 40–50 min ○ Mix cheese and cream, and, spread over flat side of potatoes. Sprinkle with caraway seeds ○ Return to oven for another 5–10 min.

Preparation time 60 minutes

Serves 4

Eat with chicory salad.

POTATO SUBMARINE

Ingredients

8 baking potatoes, medium size

100 g (4 oz) lambs liver, chopped

1 onion, finely chopped

2 cloves of garlic, finely chopped

100 g (4 oz) lamb mince

2 tbsp. butter

salt

black pepper, freshly ground

100 g (4 oz) Cheddar cheese, grated

for greasing: oil

Preparation

○ Brush 8 sheets of foil with some oil ○ Wash potatoes and pat dry ○ Slice tops off the potatoes and scoop out, leaving a thin shell. (Discard scooped out tops) ○ Chop potato flesh finely ○ Melt butter, fry onion and garlic until translucent ○ Add potato flesh, liver, mince and continue frying for about 5 min. Season with salt and pepper ○ Preheat oven to 220°C/425°F/Gas Mark 7 ○ Spoon mixture back into potato shells and top with cheese ○ Wrap loosely in prepared foil ○ Bake for 50–60 min.

Preparation time 1 hour 30 minutes

Serves 4

Very good with a cauliflower salad.

POTATO TUNA BOAT

Ingredients

4 large baking potatoes
1 tin of white tuna, flaked
25 g (1 oz) butter
1 carton soured cream
salt
black pepper, freshly
ground

100 g (4 oz) Cheddar
cheese, grated
1 bag of crisps (ready
salted)

Preparation

○ Preheat oven to 180°C/350°F/Gas Mark 4 ○ Wash potatoes and place in oven. Bake for about 1½–2 hours, or until just tender ○ Slice tops off the potatoes and scoop out, leaving a thin shell. (Discard scooped out tops) ○ Mash potato flesh, mix with tuna (incl. oil), butter and cream. Season with salt and pepper ○ Spoon mixture back into potato shells ○ Crumble crisps and mix with cheese. Top potatoes ○ Place potatoes on a baking tray and return to oven ○ Bake for about 20 min. at 200°C/400°F/Gas Mark 6.

Preparation time 2 hours 30 minutes

Serves 4

Try it with a cucumber and yoghurt salad.

POTATOES FILLED WITH ROQUEFORT CHEESE

Ingredients

8 baking potatoes, medium size
150 g (6 oz) curd cheese
150 g (6 oz) Roquefort cheese
salt
white pepper
2 tbsp. butter, soft
2 tsp. paprika
2 tbsp. fresh parsley finely chopped
for greasing: butter

Preparation

○ Wash potatoes and cook covered in salted water for about 25 min ○ Drain and allow to cool briefly ○ Slice tops off the potatoes (keep tops) and scoop out, leaving a thin shell ○ Mash potato flesh thoroughly with curd cheese, Roquefort cheese, parsley, pepper and butter ○ Spoon mixture back into potato shells and put tops back on ○ Preheat oven to 200°C/400°F/Gas Mark 6 ○ Arrange potatoes on a greased baking tray, sprinkle generously with salt and paprika, and, bake for about 10–15 min.

Preparation time 60 minutes

Serves 4

Very tasty, serve with green bean and onion salad.

POTATOES STUFFED WITH BACON

Ingredients

8 baking potatoes, medium size

2 onions, finely chopped

4 cloves of garlic, finely chopped

100 ml (4 fl oz) olive oil

1 tbsp. English mustard

200 g (8 oz) smoked streaky bacon, rindless, chopped

white pepper

salt

fresh parsley, finely chopped

Preparation

○ Preheat oven to 200°C/400°F/Gas Mark 6 ○ Wash potatoes and bake for about 50–60 min ○ Heat oil in a saucepan, add garlic and onions, fry for about 4 min. ○ Remove from heat, and stir in the mustard ○ Fry bacon (without fat) until crispy. Discard fat ○ Slice tops off the potatoes and scoop out the flesh, leaving a thin shell. (Discard tops) ○ Mash potato flesh, mix with parsley, bacon, and onion sauce. Season with salt and pepper ○ Spoon mixture back into potato shells ○ Arrange potatoes on a baking tray, and return to oven ○ Bake for another 10 min.

Preparation time 1 hour 30 minutes

Serves 4

A real treat with a cucumber salad.

POTATO NESTS

Ingredients

4 large baking potatoes	white pepper
50 g (2 oz) butter	4 eggs
salt	paprika

Preparation

○ Preheat oven to 200°C/400°F/Gas Mark 6 ○ Wash and scrub potatoes thoroughly ○ Place on a baking tray, and bake for about 1–1½ hours, or until soft ○ Cut tops off the potatoes and scoop out (discard tops), leaving a thin shell ○ Mash potato flesh with butter. Season with salt and pepper ○ Spoon mixture back into potato shells. Press a hollow ○ Break one egg into each hollow ○ Return to oven for about 5–10 min. ○ Serve sprinkled with paprika.

Preparation time 1 hour 45 minutes

Serves 4

Serve with ham and baked beans.

CHEESY SOUFFLÉ POTATOES

Ingredients

4 large baking potatoes	3 egg yolks
100 g (4 oz) Cheddar cheese, grated	3 egg whites, whipped stiff
	salt
4 tsp. English mustard	white pepper
25 g (1 oz) butter, soft	

Preparation

○ Preheat oven to 200°C/400°F/Gas Mark 6 ○ Wash and dry potatoes and place in oven. Bake for about 1–1½ hours, or until tender ○ Slice tops off the potatoes and scoop out, leaving a thin shell. (Discard scooped out tops) ○ Mash potato flesh, mix with butter, mustard, egg yolks and cheese. Season with salt and pepper ○ Fold the whipped egg whites gently into the potato mixture ○ Spoon mixture back into potato shells ○ Place potatoes on a baking tray and return to oven ○ Bake for about 10–15 min., or until risen and golden.

Preparation time 2 hours

Serves 4

Very nice with tomato and onion salad.

FOIL POTATOES
Basic preparation for 4 portions

Ingredients

4 large baking potatoes   1 tsp. salt
1 tbsp. oil

Preparation

○ Preheat oven to 220°C/425°F/Gas Mark 7 ○ Wash potatoes thoroughly and pat dry ○ Cut four pieces of foil (sufficient for wrapping) ○ Brush each foil with oil and sprinkle with salt and caraway seeds ○ Wrap potatoes and bake for about 1–1½ hours, depending on size ○ Unwrap, cut crosswise, add topping or dip and serve.

On the following pages, I am going to mention, just a few of my favourite toppings, and dips. There are however, no restrictions to your desires! YOU can create your own special combinations!

All recipes for toppings and dips are for 4 servings.

TUNA – MAYONNAISE

Ingredients

1 tin of light meat tuna, flaked, drained
1 small onion, finely chopped
2 tomatoes, finely diced
5 tbsp. mayonnaise, from a jar

1 tbsp. white wine vinegar
salt
black pepper, freshly ground
1 tbsp. fresh chives, finely chopped

Preparation

○ Combine tuna, onion and tomatoes ○ Add mayonnaise and vinegar. Mix well. Season with salt and pepper ○ Divide mixture between potatoes ○ Serve sprinkled with chives.

SMOKED MACKEREL AND HORSERADISH CREAM

Ingredients

2 large smoked mackerel fillets, flaked
2 small onions, finely chopped
1 tbsp. fresh parsley, finely chopped

black pepper, freshly ground
4 tbsp. horseradish cream, from a jar
4 green olives, chopped

Preparation

○Combine mackerels, onions, parsley and horseradish cream. Season with pepper. Mix well ○ Divide mixture between potatoes ○ Top each one with chopped olives.

FRANKFURTER AND BEANS

Ingredients

4 Frankfurters, sliced   1 can of baked beans
1 medium onion, finely   1 tbsp. oil
chopped

Preparation

○ Heat oil and sauté onion until translucent ○ Add
Frankfurters and baked beans. Simmer for about 10 min.
Stir occasionally ○ Divide mixture between potatoes.

RATATOUILLE AND CHEESE

Ingredients

100 g (4 oz) Cheddar   1 can of ratatouille
cheese, grated

Preparation

○ Heat ratatouille thoroughly ○ Divide mixture between
potatoes ○ Top each potato with cheese and grill for a few
minutes.

CHIVES AND CREAM CHEESE

Ingredients

200 g (8 oz) cream cheese   salt
4 tbsp. chives, chopped

Preparation

○ Combine cream cheese and chives. Mix well and season with salt ○ Divide mixture between potatoes.

BACON AND EGGS

Ingredients

200 g (8 oz) streaky bacon,
rindless, chopped
4 eggs
1 tsp. oil
salt

black pepper, freshly
ground
fresh parsley, finely
chopped

Preparation

○ Heat oil in a frying pan, and sauté bacon until crispy
○ Add eggs stirring constantly and season with salt and
pepper ○ Do not allow mixture to settle too much ○
Divide mixture between potatoes ○ Serve sprinkled with
parsley.

HAM AND SALAD CREAM

Ingredients

4 slices of cooked ham,
diced
2 tomatoes, chopped
5 tbsp. salad cream

1 hard-boiled egg,
chopped

Preparation

○ Combine ham, tomatoes and salad cream. Mix gently
○ Divide mixture between potatoes ○ Top with chopped
egg.

CHEESE AND ONION

Ingredients

200 g (8 oz) Emmental   2 small onions, finely
cheese, grated   chopped

Preparation

○ Mix cheese and onions ○ Divide mixture between potatoes ○ Grill until cheese starts melting.

WALNUT AND STILTON

Ingredients

150 g (6 oz) Stilton,   ½ small carton single
crumbled   cream
50 (2 oz) walnuts, finely
chopped

Preparation

○ Combine all ingredients and stir gently ○ Divide mixture between potatoes.

TOMATO AND CURD CHEESE

Ingredients

250 g (10 oz) curd cheese   1 tsp. paprika
½ small carton single   ½ tsp. chilli sauce
cream   salt
2 tbsp. tomato ketchup

Preparation

○ Blend all ingredients and season with salt ○ Divide mixture between potatoes.

CUCUMBER AND CURD CHEESE

Ingredients

250 g (10 oz) curd cheese	salt
1 small carton single cream	black pepper, freshly
1 clove of garlic, crushed	ground
½ cucumber, peeled,	minced garlic, dried
finely diced	

Preparation

○ Whisk curd cheese and cream until smooth ○ Add garlic and cucumber. Season with salt and pepper and mix well ○ Divide mixture between potatoes ○ Serve sprinkled with minced garlic.

SAVOURY BUTTER

Ingredients

125 g (5 oz) butter, soft	1 tsp. fresh parsley, finely
½ tsp. lemon juice	chopped
½ tsp. paprika	salt
1 clove of garlic, crushed	black pepper, freshly
½ tbsp. capers, finely	ground
chopped	

Preparation

○ Whisk butter, and, add all ingredients. Season with salt and pepper. ○ On a foil form a roll and wrap. Place in the refrigerator until hard ○ Cut into slices before serving.

WATERCRESS CREAM

Ingredients

250 g (10 oz) curd cheese
1 small carton single cream
4 tbsp. watercress, finely chopped

2 cloves of garlic, crushed
salt
black pepper, freshly ground

Preparation

○ Whisk curd cheese and cream until smooth ○ Add watercress and garlic. Season with salt and pepper and mix well ○ Divide mixture between potatoes.

BEETROOT CREAM

Ingredients

1 carton soured cream
15 slices of pickled beetroot, finely chopped
4 tbsp. mayonnaise, from a jar

4 tbsp. horseradish cream, from a jar
2 cloves garlic, crushed
white pepper
salt

Preparation

○ Mix all ingredients. Season with salt and pepper ○ Divide mixture between potatoes.

MUSTARD AND HERB

Ingredients

250 g (10 oz) curd cheese
1 small carton single cream
2 tbsp. mustard, mild
½ tsp. Worcestershire sauce
1 tsp. fresh parsley, finely
chopped

1 tsp. fresh chives, finely
chopped
1 tsp. fresh watercress,
finely chopped

Preparation

○ Whisk curd cheese and cream until smooth ○ Add all ingredients and mix well. Chill for about 30 min. ○ Divide mixture between potatoes.

PRAWN – MAYONNAISE

Ingredients

200 g (8 oz) prawns
4 tbsp. mayonnaise, from a jar
4 tbsp. single cream
2 tbsp. tomato ketchup

1 tsp. Worcestershire sauce
½ tsp. lemon juice
salt
white pepper

Preparation

○ Combine mayonnaise, single cream, tomato ketchup, lemon juice and Worcestershire sauce. Season with salt and pepper ○ Add prawns and mix well ○ Divide mixture between potatoes.

EGGS AND CHIVES

Ingredients

4 hard-boiled eggs, coarsely diced
4 tbsp. mayonnaise, from a jar
6 tbsp. single cream

2 cloves of garlic, crushed
2 tbsp. fresh chives, finely chopped
salt
white pepper

Preparation

○ Combine mayonnaise, single cream, garlic and chives. Season with salt and pepper ○ Add eggs and toss gently ○ Divide mixture between potatoes.

BEEF AND SPRING ONION

Ingredients

150 g (6 oz) cooked beef, cut into strips
6 spring onions, finely sliced
4 tbsp. mayonnaise, from a jar

4 tbsp. single cream
½ tsp. Worcestershire sauce
salt
black pepper, freshly ground

Preparation

○ Combine mayonnaise, single cream and Worcestershire sauce. Season with salt and pepper ○ Add beef and spring onions. Mix well ○ Divide mixture between potatoes.

ANCHOVY AND GARLIC

Ingredients

1 tin of anchovies fillets, drained, finely chopped
250 g (10 oz) curd cheese
1 small carton natural yoghurt

4 cloves of garlic, crushed
1 tsp. fresh parsley, finely chopped
black pepper, freshly ground

Preparation

○ Blend curd cheese and yoghurt until smooth ○ Add anchovies, garlic and parsley. Season with pepper ○ Divide mixture between potatoes.

PAPRIKA AND CHEESE

Ingredients

250 g (10 oz) cottage cheese, plain
6 cocktail gherkins, finely chopped
1 tsp. paprika

cayenne pepper, pinch
½ tsp. caraway seeds
salt
white pepper

Preparation

○ Combine all ingredients and mix well. Season with salt and pepper ○ Divide mixture between potatoes.

PISTACHIO AND HAM

Ingredients

250 g (10 oz) cottage cheese

50 g (2 oz) cooked ham,
finely diced

50 g (2 oz) pistachio,

chopped

salt

white pepper

Preparation

○ Combine all ingredients and mix well. Season with salt
and pepper ○ Divide mixture between potatoes.

YOGHURT AND APPLE

Ingredients

2 small cartons natural
yoghurt

100 g (4 oz) Red Leicester
cheese, grated

2 eating apples, unpeeled,
cored, finely diced

1 tbsp. walnuts, chopped

Preparation

○ Combine all ingredients and mix well ○ Divide mixture between potatoes.

SOURED CREAM AND CHEESE

Ingredients

2 cartons soured cream
150 g (6 oz) mature
Cheddar cheese, grated

1 tbsp. fresh chives, finely
chopped

Preparation

○ Combine all ingredients and mix well ○ Divide mixture between potatoes.

BLACK PUDDING AND ONION

Ingredients

300 g (12 oz) black
pudding, diced

1 onion, finely chopped
1 tbsp. oil

Preparation

○ Heat oil in a frying pan and sauté onion until translucent ○ Add black pudding and continue frying until almost crispy ○ Divide mixture between potatoes.

LUMPFISH ROE (CAVIAR) & COTTAGE CHEESE

Ingredients

1 small jar of lumpfish roe
200 g (8 oz) cottage cheese
3 hard-boiled eggs,
chopped

salt
black pepper, freshly
ground

Preparation

○ Season cottage cheese with salt and pepper ○ Add chopped eggs and mix gently ○ Divide mixture between potatoes ○ Sprinkle each portion generously with lumpfish roe

Desserts

POTATO PLUM DUMPLINGS

Ingredients

1 kg (2 lb) floury	6 tbsp. butter
potatoes	5 tbsp. breadcrumbs,
2 egg yolks	natural
1 tsp. salt	icing sugar
250 g (10 oz) plain flour	approx. 12 fresh plums
2–3 tbsp. oil	

Preparation

○ Wash potatoes and cook covered in salted water for about 25–30 min., or until tender ○ Drain and allow to cool briefly ○ Peel, and, mash immediately ○ Mix mash with egg yolks, salt, oil and flour ○ Knead a dough, if still sticky add some more flour ○ Between floured hands flatten a piece of dough and wrap a plum (wiped dry) into it. Forming a firm dumpling ○ Repeat procedure ○ Bring approx. 4 pints of salted water to the boil ○ Add dumplings, which should be able to float and be slightly submerged ○ Cook for about 10–12 min ○ In a large frying pan melt the butter and brown breadcrumbs, set aside ○ Remove dumplings with a slotted spoon and toss carefully in butter and breadcrumb mixture ○ Serve warm dusted with icing sugar.

Preparation time 60 minutes

Serves 4–6

You can change plums for apricots or even strawberries

A lovely dessert.

POTATO NOODLES WITH APPLE PURÉE

Ingredients

1 kg (2 lb) floury
potatoes
2 egg yolks
1 tsp. salt
250 g (10 oz) plain flour

2–3 tbsp. oil
500 ml (1 pint) apple
purée, from a jar
whipping cream

Preparation

○ Wash potatoes and cook covered in salted water for about 25–30 min., or until tender ○ Drain and allow to cool briefly ○ Peel and mash immediately ○ Mix potatoes with egg yolks, salt, oil and flour ○ Form a dough, if still sticky add some more flour ○Between floured hands form little noodles (1 inch long) ○ Bring approx. 4 pints of salted water to the boil ○ Add noodles, which should be able to float and be slightly submerged ○ Cook for about 10–12 min. ○ Lift out with a slotted spoon, place into individual bowls, top with apple purée and whipping cream ○ Serve warm.

Prepartation time 1 hour 15 minutes

Serves 4–6

Simple but refreshing.

POTATO RAISIN BURGERS

Ingredients

500 g (1 lb) floury
potatoes
2 tbsp. butter, soft
75 g (3 oz) sugar
2 eggs
salt, pinch

rind of whole lemon,
grated
250 g (10 oz) curd cheese
2–3 tbsp. plain flour
50 g (2 oz) raisins
for frying: 4 tbsp. suet

Preparation the day before

○ Wash potatoes and cook covered in salted water for about 25–30 min. ○ Drain and place in a bowl or dish overnight. Do not refrigerate.

Preparation following day

○Peel potatoes and grate into a bowl ○ Whisk butter, sugar and eggs. Mix with salt, lemon rind and curd cheese. Add potatoes, flour, raisins and form a dough ○ With floured hands shape into burgers ○ Heat suet and fry for about 15 min. or until golden on both sides ○ Eat hot!

Preparation time 60 minutes

Serves 4–6

Lovely with stewed fruit.

POTATO SCONES

Ingredients

500 g (1 lb) floury potatoes	75–100 g (3–4 oz) wholemeal flour
25 g (1 oz) butter	3 tbsp. oil

Preparation

○ Wash potatoes and cook covered in salted water for about 25–30 min., or until tender ○ Drain and peel immediately ○ Mash thoroughly ○ Add butter, and work in enough flour to make a stiff dough ○ Roll out on a floured surface to ½ inch thickness ○ Cut into rounds with a pastry cutter ○ Heat oil and fry over a medium heat for about 4–5 min. on each side ○ Serve warm.

Preparation time 60 minutes

Serves 4

Serve dusted with sugar and accompanied by stewed apples.

GNOCCHI IN CHOCOLATE SAUCE

Ingredients

500 g (1 lb) floury
potatoes
1 egg
100 g (4 oz) plain flour

salt, pinch
chocolate sauce, from a jar
whipping cream

Preparation the day before

○ Wash potatoes and cook covered in salted water for about 25–30 min. or until tender ○ Drain and allow to cool briefly ○ Peel, and, mash thoroughly ○ Add beaten egg and salt. Mix well ○ Add flour using your hands ○ Spread smooth dough on a floured surface, and cut into small squares ○ Roll each square and flatten slightly ○ In a large pan bring salted water to the boil ○ Drop in gnocchi and cook until they float ○ Lift out with a slotted spoon ○ Pour over chocolate sauce and top with whipping cream ○ Serve warm.

Preparation time 60 minutes

Serves 4–6

An unusual dessert.

CINNAMON LATKES

Ingredients

1 kg (2 lb) floury potatoes	1 tsp. ground cinnamon
50 g (2 oz) caster sugar	1 egg, slightly beaten
50 g (2 oz) self-raising flour	icing sugar
	for frying: oil

Preparation

○ Wash and peel potatoes ○ Grate potatoes, and, squeeze through a muslin cloth until completely dry ○ Place in a bowl, add flour, cinnamon, sugar and egg. Mix thoroughly ○ Heat oil in a large frying pan and spread a tablespoon of mixture at a time, continue procedure ○ Fry latkes for about 5–8 min., turning once, until golden brown ○ Serve dusted with icing sugar.

Preparation time 45 minutes

Serves 4–6

Equally nice – hot or cold!.

Appendices

COMPOSITION OF THE RAW POTATO

78.8 % Water
15.6 % Starch
 1.7 % Fibre

2.1 % Protein
1.3 % Sugar
0.2 % Fat

0.02 % Vitamins (which are water soluble):

Vit. C (Ascorbic Acid)	– Present in all body tissues. Aids healing of skin and bones. Stress and cold increase the need for it.
Vit. B_2(Riboflavin)	– For growth and various tissues.
Vit. B_6(Pyridoxine)	– Helps make red blood cells.

0.8 % Minerals and Trace Elements:

Potassium	– Used in body cells. Vital for muscles. Particularly the heart muscles.
Iodine	– Vital for the thyroid gland.
Iron	– Used for making red blood cells, which carry oxygen.
Calcium	– Used in muscles, nerves, certain hormones and enzymes but most of all in bones.
Copper	– Enables the body to use iron, needed for some enzymes to work.

ENERGY COMPARISON OF 100 g PORTIONS

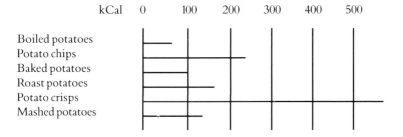

Potatoes contain only 23 calories per 25 g (1 ounce), when served boiled. On average we each eat approx. 110 kg (242 lb) potatoes every year.

Information regarding varieties of potatoes, nutritional, and other technical data, kindly supplied by the Potato Marketing Board.

HELPFUL HINTS AND TIPS

○ Always treat potatoes with care, because they bruise easily.

○ Always remove potatoes from their polythene bag, to avoid sweating.

○ Always store potatoes in the dark, because light turns them green.

○ Always store potatoes in a cool place, but not below 4°C (40°F), as frost changes their chemistry unpleasantly.

○ Always peel potatoes thinly, to preserve nutrients, which are just under the skin.

○ Use a potato peeler which rotates on its handle, because it removes the thinnest layer of skin.

○ When you peel raw potatoes you have approx. 20 % wasteage, compared with 4–6 % when they are cooked.

○ Always cut potatoes into equal-sized pieces, to ensure even cooking.

○ Cook potaotes steadily, remember a potato boiled, is a potato spoiled.

○ Cook potatoes in the smallest amount of water possible and drain immediately, because Vit. C dissolves in water.

○ Cook potatoes in a microwave, if possible. The potato will retain more Vit. C.

○ New potatoes cook best, when put into boiling water.

○ Maincrop potatoes cook more evenly, if put into cold water and brought to the boil.

○ When potatoes go green, that area tastes unpleasant and contains a poison called Solanine. Cut out all green parts, and the rest will be safe to eat.

○ Do not worry if potatoes have a purple patch on it, this is just a natural vegetable colour.

○ Potaotes go black/grey when cooked, if they have a high level of iron. To reduce this reaction, just add vinegar or lemon juice to the cooking water.

○ Use the potato water for gravy, or as the liquid in soups.

○ Toss sauté potatoes in flour before frying, it enhances the colour.

○ Use kitchen gloves, where a recipe suggests the potatoes be cooked in their skin, and, peeled whist still hot/warm.

Index

Illustrations are indicated by *italic* numerals. Section titles are set in SMALL CAPITALS.

L

latkes, cinnamon 116
layers, potato Gouda
cheese 81
leek soup, potato and 22
lentil soup, potato and 16
lumpfish roe and cottage
cheese filling for foil
potatoes 108
lyonnaise potatoes 48

M

MAIN COURSES 63–86
mackerel, smoked, and
horseradish cream filling
for foil potatoes 97
mash, potato and onion 58
mashed potatoes 51
minty potatoes 59
mushroom pie, potato 70
mustard and herb filling for
foil potatoes 103

N

nests, potato 93
noodles, potato, with apple
purée 112
nut balls, potato 53

O

olive oil, potatoes in 55

omelette, potato 66
omelette, potato and corned
beef *61*, 72
onion, potato and, mash 58

P

panfried potatoes with
prawns 71
paprika, potatoes in 60
paprika and cheese filling for
foil potatoes 105
parsley cakes, potato *12*, *13*
parsley potatoes 54
pepper potato mix *40*, 41
pie, cottage 79
pie, potato 73
pie, potato and anchovy 68
pie,
potato mushroom 70
potato tomato 82
shepherd's 77
pistachio and ham filling for
foil potatoes 106
plum dumplings, potato 111
pommes duchesse 42
pot, potato veal 67
prawn mayonnaise filling for
foil potatoes 103
prawns, panfried potatoes
with 71
prawns, potato salad
with 32, *33*

V

veal pot, potato 67

W

walnut and stilton filling for
    foil potatoes 100
watercress cream filling for
    foil potatoes 102

Y

yoghurt and apple filling for
    foil potatoes 106

Z

Zürcher Rösti 75